What Do You Call a Baby Rhino?
And Other Baby Mammals

EMMA NATHAN

BLACKBIRCH PRESS, INC.

WOODBRIDGE, CONNECTICUT

Published by Blackbirch Press, Inc.
260 Amity Road
Woodbridge, CT 06525
web site: http://www.blackbirch.com
e-mail: staff@blackbirch.com

Printed in Singapore

10 9 8 7 6 5 4 3 2 1

Photo Credits
Cover and title page: ©PhotoDisc; pages 3, 5, 6, 8, 10-12, 14, 20, 22: ©Corel
Corporation; pages 7, 8 (silhouette), 9, 13, 17-19, 20 (silhouette), 21:
©PhotoDisc; page 15: ©D. Parer & E. Parer-Cook/Peter Arnold; page 16:
©K. Atkinson/OSF/Animals Animals.

Library of Congress Cataloging-in-Publication Data
Nathan, Emma.
        What do you call a baby rhino? : and other baby mammals / Emma
Nathan.—1st. ed.
                        p. cm.—(What do you call a baby—)
        Includes bibliographical references. (p.   )
        Summary: Provides the special names for such baby mammals as
the fawn, joey, and puppy, describing their physical characteristics, behavior,
and treatment by their parents.
        ISBN 1-56711-364-8
        1. Mammals—Infancy—Juvenile literature.[1. Mammals.
2. Animals—Infancy. 3. Parental behavior in animals.] I. Title. II. Series:
Nathan, Emma. What do you call a baby—
QL706.2.N34   1999   99-20250
599.13'9—dc21   CIP
                                                                AC

Contents

What do you call a baby rhino?

De-Calf (with Milk)

A rhino mother has a baby every 3 to 4 years. Only 1 calf is born at a time. On average, a calf will nurse for about 2 years—even though it can eat regular food much earlier. When it is full grown, a rhino can reach a length of 14 feet (4 meters) or more. It can also weigh up to 6,000 pounds (2,720 kilograms), which is the average weight of 35 men!

A baby rhino is called a calf.

What do you call a baby seal **?**

Puppy Love

Harp seals give birth to their pups in the spring. A typical seal mother will give birth to one pup at a time, but twins are common. Before giving birth, a seal will swim far away to find a quiet spot in a frozen bay. This protects her new-born pup from hungry polar bears and other predators. At her spot, she will make a hole in the ice. When she is ready, she will climb up onto the ice and give birth.

A baby seal is called a pup or a beach weaner.

What do you call a baby beaver**?**

••WHAT DO YOU KNOW?••

Beaver Fever

Beavers like to live in groups of families, called colonies. When a kitten is born, it stays with its family until it is fully grown. A beaver is not fully developed until it is between 2 to 3 years old. At that point, it can weigh as much as 60 pounds (27 kilograms) and can hold its breath underwater for about 30 minutes. An adult beaver can also bring down a tree up to 42 inches (106 centimeters) in diameter by gnawing away at the base of the trunk!

A baby beaver is called a kitten.

What do you call a baby deer?

WHAT DO YOU KNOW?

Deer Me

Most female deer give birth to one fawn at a time. Young fawns are born with spotted coats, but the spots later disappear. A baby deer is called a fawn while it is still nursing and still has its spots. An adult can run up to 40 miles per hour (64 kilometers per hour) and can jump 15 to 20 feet (6 meters) at once. Full-grown males lose their antlers every year, but they regrow them. As they grow in, they are covered with a soft velvet-like hair.

A baby deer is called a fawn.

What do you call a baby dog?

Lend a Whelping Hand

Baby dogs are born blind and deaf. It is only after a few weeks that they are fully able to use all their senses. A puppy is any dog less than 1 year old. A whelp is a puppy that has not been weaned (is still nursing). Dogs were probably the first animals tamed by humans about 10,000 years ago. Today, there are an estimated 150 million dogs in the world—more than 400 different breeds.

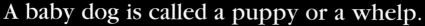

A baby dog is called a puppy or a whelp.

What do you call a baby zebra?

The Foal Goal

After a year-long pregnancy, a mother zebra gives birth to her foal in the spring. From the moment it is born, a foal can stand and even run. It can also recognize its mother by her scent. Young foals live together in a group with other members of a herd. Even though it is hard for most people to tell one zebra from another, each animal has a unique stripe pattern—one as unique as a human fingerprint.

What do you call a baby echidna?

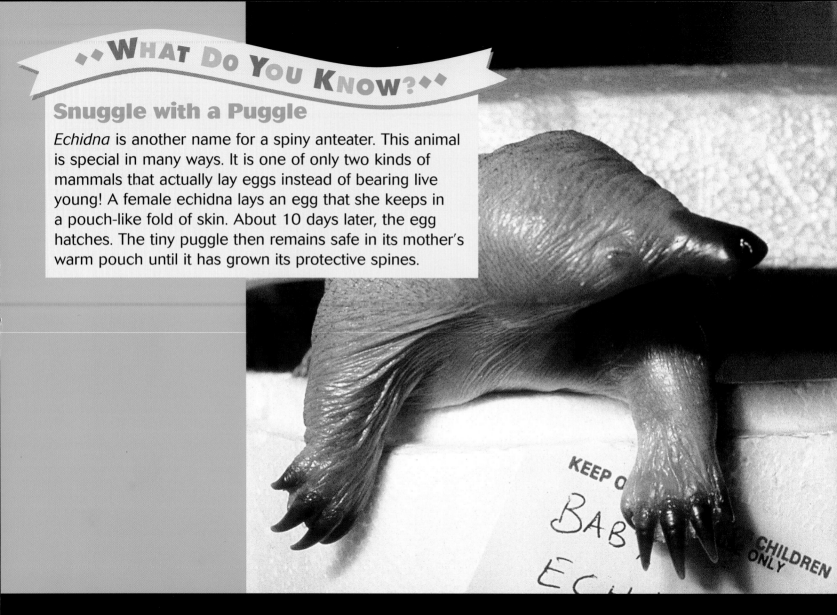

Snuggle with a Puggle

Echidna is another name for a spiny anteater. This animal is special in many ways. It is one of only two kinds of mammals that actually lay eggs instead of bearing live young! A female echidna lays an egg that she keeps in a pouch-like fold of skin. About 10 days later, the egg hatches. The tiny puggle then remains safe in its mother's warm pouch until it has grown its protective spines.

KEEP O

BAB

ECH

CHILDREN ONLY

A baby echidna is called a puggle.

What do you call a baby lion?

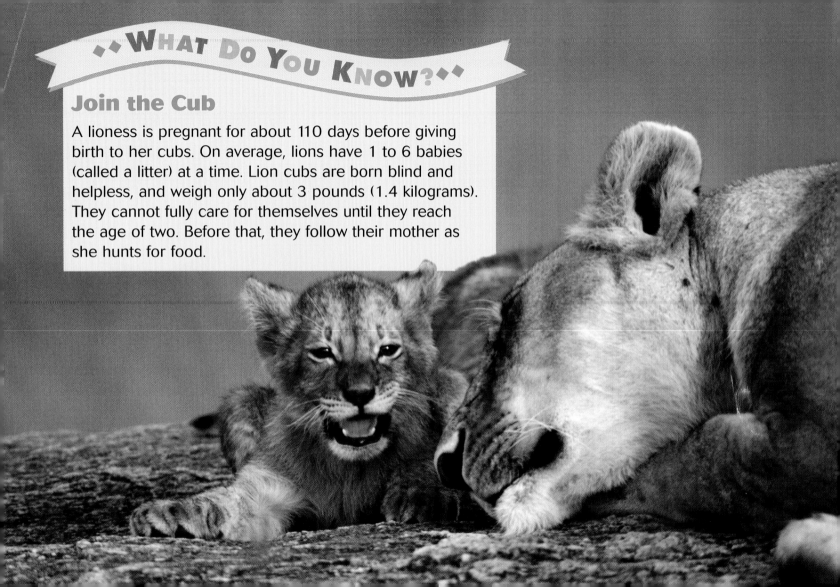

Join the Cub

A lioness is pregnant for about 110 days before giving birth to her cubs. On average, lions have 1 to 6 babies (called a litter) at a time. Lion cubs are born blind and helpless, and weigh only about 3 pounds (1.4 kilograms). They cannot fully care for themselves until they reach the age of two. Before that, they follow their mother as she hunts for food.

What do you call a baby kangaroo?

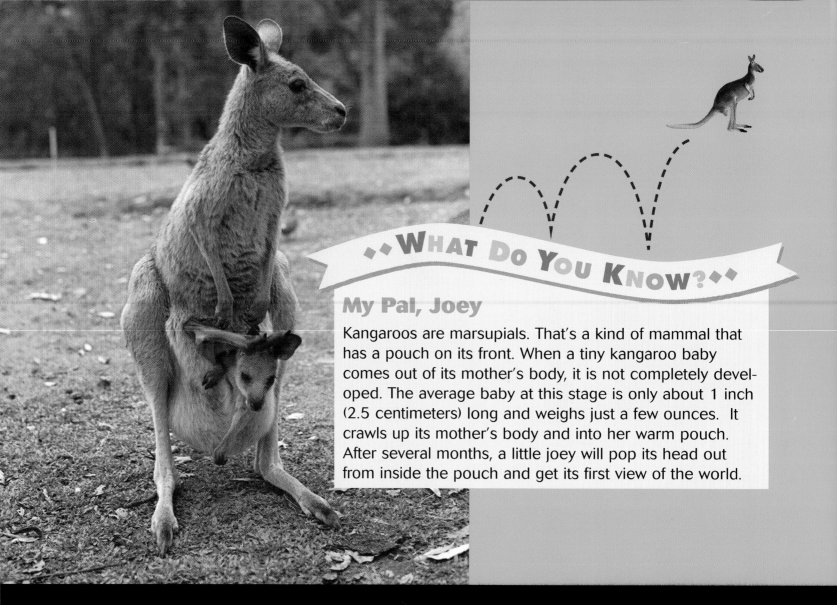

My Pal, Joey

Kangaroos are marsupials. That's a kind of mammal that has a pouch on its front. When a tiny kangaroo baby comes out of its mother's body, it is not completely developed. The average baby at this stage is only about 1 inch (2.5 centimeters) long and weighs just a few ounces. It crawls up its mother's body and into her warm pouch. After several months, a little joey will pop its head out from inside the pouch and get its first view of the world.

A baby kangaroo is called a joey.

What do you call a baby raccoon?

Do-It-Yourself Kit

When kits are born, their masks and tail rings can hardly be seen and their eyes are closed. By the time they are 7 weeks old, they are running, climbing, and making sounds almost as well as adults. Unlike other mammals, kits will overeat when nursing, so mother raccoons need to know when enough is enough!

A baby raccoon is called a kit.

Some Other Baby Mammals

Calf	Pup	Kitten	Fawn	Whelp	Foal
rhino	*seal*	*beaver*	*deer*	*dog*	*zebra*
bison	aardvark	mouse	pronghorn	otter	donkey
camel	anteater	cat	moose	tiger	horse
cattle	bat	squirrel		wolf	mule
elephant	coyote	porcupine			
giraffe	dolphin				
hippo	gerbil				
ibex	hyena				
reindeer					

			Joey	Kit	Cub
			kangaroo	*raccoon*	*lion*
			koala	badger	bear
			opossum	skunk	leopard
			wallaby	weasel	
			wombat	fox	

Glossary

Antlers—two large, branching, bony structures on the head of a deer or moose that are shed and regrown.

Breed—a type of species with characteristics that set it apart from other members of the species.

Colonies—large groups of animals that live, feed, and travel together.

Develop—to grow larger and stronger, taking on adult characteristics.

Herd—a large number of animals of the same species located in one place, or moving together as a group.

Marsupial—the name for a group of animals in which the females carry their developing young in a pouch on their abdomen.

Nurse—to feed young mammals milk from their mother's body.

Predators—animals that live by hunting other animals for food.

Senses—the five senses are sight, taste, smell, touch, and hearing.

Tamed—taken from the wild or natural state and trained to live with or be useful to people.

Velvet—soft skin that covers the growing antlers of a deer or moose.

Weaned—no longer nursing.

For More Information

Books

Butterworth, Christine. *Deer*. Chatham, NJ: Steck-Vaughn Library, 1990.

Ling, Mary. Gordon Clayton (Photographer). *Foal* (See How They Grow). New York, NY: DK Publishing, 1992.

Owen, Oliver S. *Cub to Grizzly Bear* (Lifewatch). Minneapolis, MN: Abdo & Daughters, 1996.

Petty, Kate. *Baby Animals: Seals.* Hauppauge, NY: Barron Educational Series, 1992.

Ryden, Hope. *Joey: The Story of a Baby Kangaroo.* New York, NY: William Morrow, 1994.

Tesar, Jenny. *What On Earth Is an Echidna?* (What on Earth). Woodbridge, CT: Blackbirch Press, Inc.), 1995.

Web Sites

Animal Bytes
Information on unique creatures in the animal kingdom—www.seaworld.org/animal_bytes/animal_bytes.html

The Rhino
A ton of rhino facts, including information on poaching—www.dscf.demon.co.uk/fact1.html

The World Wide Raccoon Web
Great raccoon facts, photographs, news, and links—www.loomcom.com/raccoons

Wild Discovery—Marsupials
The Discovery Channel features the lifestyle of the kangaroo—www.tlc.discovery.com/conv/wilddiscovery/wilddiscovery980302/weblinks.html

Index